HIDDEN TREASURE

Amherst Sunrise Church of the Nazarene

HIDDEN TREASURE

MARION K. RICH

Beacon Hill Press of Kansas City
Kansas City, Missouri

Copyright 1988, 1993, 1998
by Beacon Hill Press of Kansas City

New Edition 1998

Printed in the
United States of America

lSBN 083-411-2264

Cover Design: Paul Franitza
Cover Illustration: NPH
Illustrated by Don Fields

Note: This book is part of the *Understanding Christian Mission* curriculum. It is designed for use in Year III, Compassionate Ministries. This study year examines our responsibility to minister to all the needs of people around the world —physical, mental, emotional, and spiritual.

10   9   8   7   6   5   4   3   2   1

Contents

1.

A Strange Discovery

"Quiet, Fifi (FEE-fee)!" ordered Stephen, the tall, slim, Haitian lad. He reached down to pat his restless, growling dog.

But Fifi heard the sound of feet rustling through the bushes. She cocked her head and barked more excitedly than ever.

"Fifi, what is it?" Stephen asked.

He followed Fifi a short distance through a clearing. The dog began sniffing the ground.

It was already too late to be so far away from his house. He should not have wandered away from his own yard. Would anyone miss him? The darkness seemed especially thick and velvety. Stephen began to feel uneasy—as if unfriendly spirits were watching.

Fifi started off through the bushes.

"Wait," whispered Stephen. "Don't leave me!"

The dog began to act strangely. Twice she paused to sniff the air and whine. Once she looked up into Stephen's face and growled as if trying to tell him something. Then she darted out of the bushes.

"Fifi, what is it?" Stephen asked again.

She gazed alertly about the clearing. It was deserted, yet every rustle of the leaves seemed to warn him to be careful. Fifi began to sniff and tug at something. The dog had led Stephen to a hollow place in the ground that was hidden by bushes.

Stooping down, the lad felt the soft earth with his hand. The dirt had been freshly dug. Something had just been buried.

Fifi lost no time. She sank her paws into the soft dirt and began digging for whatever had been buried. Dirt flew in every direction.

"Let's get out of here, Fifi," Stephen urged. "We'll come back tomorrow."

The darkness and woods bothered him. He felt that spirits were watching. Why, he might even encounter a blood-sucking vampire, he thought.

Suddenly Fifi struck something metal. It sounded like a chain.

Stephen's body seemed to tighten. He realized that danger might be lurking nearby. Wasting no further time, Stephen stumbled toward the trail. Fifi sniffed the ground, then took up the lead.

They soon reached the edge of the familiar hill and started up the winding path toward Stephen's house.

In his yard candles burned uncertainly. Dancing, swaying figures moved toward the flickering lights. The throbbing drums seemed to echo his pounding heart.

Stephen's father and mother, a voodoo priest and priestess, were busy with a voodoo ceremony. No one had missed him. Stephen felt relieved and safe. If only he could forget about the buried items in the bushes. Cautiously he slipped under the brush arbor in front of his house and sat down on the ground.

Weary, Stephen felt his body relax and his eyes close. Fifi snuggled her skinny body close to Stephen.

Soon both were asleep. Stephen never remembered when his father led him to his banana-leaf mat after the voodoo ceremony was over.

2

Startling News

The chatter of voices from the merchants going to market awakened Stephen early. Immediately he thought of the strange discovery he and Fifi had made the night before. Had anyone seen them? Should he go back today and examine the buried items?

The aroma of strong Haitian coffee filled the three-room house. Stephen's older sister, Agnes, was already in the outdoor thatched-roof kitchen. His mother, a small, kind woman with a low voice, was giving orders.

Stephen yawned, then stretched his long, thin arms. He got to his feet and rolled up the banana-leaf mat that was his bed. Setting it outside, he called, *"Bonjou"* (boh-ZHOO—"good morning"), to his family.

The sun was just coming up over the hills. Shafts of light streamed through the towering coconut palms that bent over the tin roof of Stephen's house. Agnes had already swept the ground and cleared away the ashes from last night's fire. She brought Stephen a cup of black coffee and a piece of hard roll. He dipped the roll into the hot coffee and sat down on the porch near his father. Later in the morning there would be soup, avocados, and mangoes to eat.

Stephen's family always seemed to have more to eat than his friends. His father and mother did a fairly good business with their voodoo remedies. There was hardly a day that some villagers did not come to them with ailments or problems. His parents demanded a good fee for their services. Quite often people would have to bring chickens, goats, or even a cow to Mr. and Mrs. Gustave (GEE-stahv). Sometimes they were a sacrifice to the "loa" (the Haitian gods). Other times they were payment for voodoo remedies. Mr. Gustave planned for Stephen to someday take his place as the main voodoo priest in the village of Fragneau (frah-YOE).

Mr. Gustave sharpened his machete (mah-SHET, a large, broad-bladed knife).

"Get ready, Stephen," he said. "There's a lot of work to be done in the garden today."

Stephen did not want to hear that. He was thinking about returning to the buried items in the bushes. How could he get back there without anyone seeing him? He did not feel he could tell anyone about his discovery. Yet it was all he could think about.

Picking up his machete he set off through the fields with his father to the garden. The millet was ready to be harvested. Hard work now would mean there would be food to eat later.

At noon the hot sun was directly overhead. Beads of sweat dotted Stephen's bare back. The white handkerchief tied around his father's head was dripping wet.

"The heat of the day is no time to be in the garden," Mr. Gustave said. "Let's go!"

Back at his house, Stephen climbed a tall coconut palm tree. He knocked several green coconuts to the ground. With his machete he cut off the tops, making a small opening to pour the juice out of. Never had coconut juice tasted more refreshing! Stephen smacked his lips. He and his father drank until they were no longer thirsty. Then Stephen split the coconuts in two pieces with his machete. They ate the white meat inside the coconut.

Neighbors strolled by the path near Stephen's house. From time to time someone would stop in for a few minutes and tell the latest gossip.

Stephen started to slip away to the bushes to examine his discovery of the evening before. Then a neighboring voodoo priestess, riding sidesaddle on her donkey, entered the yard. She greeted the family with a broad smile. Magrit (mah-GREET) lived on the top of the hill. She was a powerful woman. Everyone for miles around knew Magrit. She wore a long-sleeved, white dress. A red sash was tied around her waist. Round, golden earrings dangled beneath her red and white, polka-dot turban.

Magrit dismounted gracefully from her donkey. Mr. Gustave stood to his feet and politely offered her a chair. Madame (mah-DAHM) Gustave left the kitchen and told Agnes to finish preparing the dinner. She drew up a small stool and warmly welcomed Magrit.

When Magrit visited she always had interesting news. "I wonder what she's going to tell us today," Stephen thought.

In hushed tones Magrit began to talk to the Gustaves. Mr. Gustave noticed Stephen's interest. He ordered the boy to fetch a bucket of water at the village fountain. Stephen had hoped all morning for a chance to get away. Now he wished he could stay. He wanted to listen to Magrit's gossip.

Slipping his feet into his sandals, Stephen picked up the water bucket near the outdoor kitchen. He stopped a moment to tease Agnes. then set out slowly along the path. He tried hard to hear what Magrit was

saying. His father clapped his hands together and gave him a look that told him he had better move along.

Could he believe what he had heard? He thought Magrit was saying something about Felix becoming the new sheriff. This was startling news!

3

A Voodoo Sacrifice

Stephen kicked a stone down the path as he balanced the bucket on his head. "It's been days since I've played soccer" he thought. He kept in the middle of the path. The sides were rough with exposed tree roots and thornbushes. Fifi walked close at his heels.

He turned from the path to a wider dirt road. On the corner was a crude brush canopy called a *tonnelle* (toh-NELL). Two crude, backless benches were underneath. Here was another place where voodoo services were held. A small, wooden cross was stuck into the ground. On it dangled a scooped-out gourd with an offering of food for a Haitian loa. The voodoo cross stands for the god of the crossroads, not for Christianity. Around the cross was a small pile of stones.

The homes along this road were mud-plastered, with palm-thatched roofs. Through open doorways Stephen saw hungry-looking children sucking on sticks of sugarcane. Families sat in their swept-out yards, weaving sisal fiber into rugs or purses, or carving pieces of mahogany. From every yard there was always the spontaneous *"Bonjou"* ("Hello"); *"Kourman ou yé?"* (koo-mah-OO-yea—"How are you?")

When Stephen arrived at the public water fountain, he met many friends. Women were washing clothes or watering their animals. Some children were bathing. Others were filling their buckets or gourds with water to take home.

Stephen chatted awhile with several friends and learned of the soccer game to be held in the afternoon. His friends urged him to be there on time.

As he was getting ready to leave, his best friend, Claude (KLOHD), arrived. Even though Claude was Stephen's age, he was much shorter. Stephen was taller and stronger than most of his friends. Maybe it was because his family was rich and always had plenty to eat.

It had been several days since Stephen and Claude had been together. There were many things to talk about. Stephen started to tell Claude about the buried articles. But then he decided to keep this secret to himself.

"Where have you been?" Stephen asked. "I looked for you at the dance in my yard last evening."

"Oh, I've been pretty busy," Claude said. "I've got a lot of things to tell you though. Will you be at the soccer game this afternoon?"

"Sure!" Stephen replied.

Claude helped Stephen lift the leaky water bucket to his head.

"I'll see you this afternoon," Claude called, as Stephen started down the road toward home.

"O revoua" (o-ray-VWAH—"So long"), shouted Stephen, gracefully balancing the water bucket.

The dripping water felt cool on Stephen's face as he hurried down the path in the hot sun.

Arriving at his yard, he noticed that Magrit was just leaving. She waved to Stephen as she started up the steep hill to her voodoo courtyard.

Dinner was ready, and Stephen was very hungry. He sat down next to his father at the wooden table. Madame Gustave lifted the screen lid that covered Stephen's tin plate. There was tasty goat meat, a large bannann (bah-NAHN) with meat sauce, and sliced, cold beets. When Stephen finished his first course he heaped his plate with rice and steaming, red bean sauce on top. What a feast! This was more than most of his friends had to eat in a week.

He quickly finished his rice and beans. Stephen's

mind flashed back to everything that happened the evening before. "If Papa would rest now," Stephen thought, "I could go back and investigate those buried articles. I might even find some money." He thought of all the things he would like to have.

He turned to his father. "You look tired, Papa. You worked hard this morning in the hot sun."

"I think I will get some rest," Mr. Gustave said. He headed for the bedroom.

Stephen flew down the path to the bushes. He was glad Fifi was asleep and did not follow him. Fifi might call attention to them if she were along. Stephen carefully looked both ways on the path to see if anyone was watching before trying to find the soft earth where he had made the discovery.

For a moment Stephen hesitated. Then he dropped to his knees and crawled into the bushes. There was no sign that Fifi had dug there the night before. Instead the dirt was carefully packed down and smoothed over. A small branch with fresh leaves had been placed over it to hide it from view. Someone had been there and repaired Stephen's and Fifi's tampering of the night before.

All of a sudden Stephen got a creepy feeling that somebody he couldn't see was watching him. He looked back over his shoulder. He tried to tell himself that his imagination was playing tricks on him.

Stephen took a deep breath. He pushed away the small branch and began to dig with his hand into the fresh dirt. His fingers felt something sharp. Clearing the dirt away he revealed the buried items; a pair of

scissors, a chain and padlock, and a bottle with some liquid carefully corked.

"Oh, no!" Stephen gasped. A voodoo sacrifice had been buried here! Spellbound, Stephen gazed down at his findings. Panic almost overwhelmed him. He must not be caught. How could he have been so stupid?

Someone had paid a voodoo priest a huge amount of money to bury this sacrifice. To meddle with it was a serious offense. Would some loa be angry with him?

Stephen's palms began to sweat. His throat tightened with fear. Hastily, he covered the items with the loose dirt and replaced the small branch. He jumped to his feet and darted out of the bushes, taking the path away from his home. He was so busy thinking about the sacrifice that he didn't notice the little old lady a few yards away who was watching him intently.

4

An Embarrassing Situation

Stephen decided to find his friend Claude and tell him about his discovery. As he neared Claude's yard he could see his friend swinging his machete through clumps of a thicket.

The two boys greeted each other warmly. Claude motioned for Stephen to sit down under the huge shade tree. Then he went to put his machete on the front porch.

From the look on Stephen's face, Claude suspected something was wrong. Stephen was glad to find Claude alone. Nervously he began to tell what had happened the past two days. He told about what he had just dug up in the bushes.

"What!" exclaimed Claude, a shocked look in his eyes. "You mean you tampered with that voodoo sacrifice? Haven't you heard?"

"Heard what?" asked Stephen.

"That's the sacrifice Felix paid Alcidas (al-SEE-das), the voodoo priest, to make in order to get his political power! Felix is the new sheriff!"

So that was what Magrit, the voodoo priestess,

was whispering to his parents that noon. If only he had heard the whole story! He would never have gone back to those bushes.

"Did anyone see you in there this afternoon?" asked Claude.

"I don't think so," Stephen replied.

"Well, you better hope Felix doesn't find out about it. He's a pretty mean character!"

"I know," said Stephen. "Why in the world does he have to be the new sheriff? Claude, do you think I've made the loa mad at me? Maybe I'll get very sick or have a terrible accident."

"Oh, I'm not so sure about that," replied Claude. "But I know if Felix finds out about it, he'll be pretty mad."

Suddenly changing his mood, Claude looked directly into Stephen's eyes. "Did you know that the Christians are not afraid of the loa?" he said quietly. "They aren't afraid of vampires, werewolves, or zombies—not even of curses put on people by the voodoo priests. They believe that Jesus Christ is their Protector."

Stephen looked interested. "How do you know about the Christians, Claude? Have you been going to their meetings?"

"Yes, I have," Claude said. "That's why I didn't come to the dance in your yard last evening. I have become a Christian."

Stephen was stunned. Before he could respond, they were interrupted. A group of boys announced that it was time for the soccer game.

Claude and Stephen stood to their feet. They and the others made their way to the field.

The soccer field was recently cleared of thornbushes. The Haitian boys had packed it down with their bare feet. They were proud of their new field. Their ball was made of a goat-skin stuffed with rags. Excitement was in the air as the game began.

Stephen's head was still swimming with the news that Claude had just told him. But as he played the game he began to feel better.

The game was nearing the end. Claude had just kicked the ball into the goal. Scores of children standing along the side of the field were cheering.

Suddenly everyone's attention was drawn to a large, brown horse galloping toward the field. The rider pulled the horse to a halt, quickly dismounted, and tied the animal to a tree.

It was Felix, the new sheriff! He was a thin, rather small man. He had a black moustache that curled upward a little at the ends. As he walked briskly toward the field, he proudly displayed his shiny new revolver. Obviously, he wanted everyone to be impressed with his authority.

The boys tried to act normally. Someone kicked the ball. As Stephen swung around, he saw Felix coming directly toward him—and he was clearly angry. Stephen didn't dare look him in the eye. But the sheriff was glaring at Stephen. He caught Stephen by the arm and jerked him roughly from the soccer game.

"Come along," he said, trembling with rage.

Stephen felt the blood rush to his cheeks.

A little girl standing by began to cry. Several children scattered in different directions. The team members watched helplessly as Stephen was led away. They

forgot about the ball and huddled together on the field.

The last thing Stephen wanted was trouble. But Felix's bad temper spelled very real trouble. Stephen tried to steady his breathing as he walked with Felix toward the path. He hoped his fear wasn't showing.

He knew he could wriggle free and run away. But he did not dare. The firm grasp of his fingers told Stephen that Felix was deadly serious. Stephen suspected that if he ran away it would only make everything worse.

Felix grabbed a long, leather whip from off his horse. He pushed Stephen on the path in the direction of his house. All Stephen could do was march forward as he was ordered. He felt both desperate and embarrassed.

5

A Severe Punishment

When they arrived at Stephen's house, Felix released his grip. Mr. and Mrs. Gustave were startled as Felix roughly pushed their son through the gate.

Felix lost no time with greetings. He launched directly into his story. There was a clear sound of authority in his voice. His taunting smile had a faint hint of a sneer.

"Who does your son think he is to try to destroy my power?" he said to Mr. Gustave. "Does he not fear the loa? Has he no respect for the law? Haven't you taught your son there is magical power in voodoo?"

Felix gestured wildly with his left arm as he spoke. He patted his gun and holster from time to time with his right hand. Stephen hung his head in shame.

Felix continued, "Twice this disorderly young man has dug up the sacrifice I have paid good money for."

Felix went on to accuse Stephen of all kinds of trickery and bad behavior that he had not done.

Stephen felt weak. He had to listen to the accusations in silence. They sounded worse and worse the more Felix talked. To deny anything the officer was saying would only make matters worse.

The more Felix talked, the fiercer Mr. Gustave's expression became. Madame Gustave was worried.

Then Felix's voice changed to a quiet, deeper more confidential tone.

"Mr. Gustave, if Stephen were anyone else's boy, I would not have waited to explain to his parents. His punishment would have already been given—and most severely! Here is my whip. I will allow you to use it on this son of yours."

Felix smiled an evil smile as Mr. Gustave took the whip. His father pushed Stephen to the corner of the yard to give him the whipping.

Madame Gustave and Agnes did not want to watch. They went into the house.

Mr. Gustave told Stephen to remove his shirt. Then he gave Stephen a kick that knocked him to his knees. As the heavy blows of the leather whip lashed across Stephen's back, he crouched lower and lower. His throat choked with sobs. He felt his eyes blur. He groaned with pain. At last it was over

Felix looked satisfied. He nodded to Mr. Gustave, tipped his hat, and started out the gate.

Back in his house, Stephen went right to bed. He lay facedown on his mat and wept quietly. He was glad to be alone. Practically in the middle of a choking sob, he fell asleep.

The next morning Stephen felt a hand gently shaking him awake. He sat up with a start. His back throbbed, reminding him of the awful day before. His mother bent over him with a tray of food. There were two biscuits, a piece of cheese, a slice of avocado, and some hot milk.

Stephen mumbled, "Thank you." He took the tray, ate the food slowly, and lay back down on his mat. He was so uncomfortable. He still felt weak.

But Stephen didn't rest well after that. He kept tossing on his banana-leaf mat, thinking over the entire unpleasant happening. He wondered if any of his friends had seen him being beaten. He wondered if this were just the beginning of his troubles. Were the loa mad at him? Would they punish him more in the days ahead? What if a vampire should visit him tonight? He trembled at these thoughts.

6

Voodoo Charms
for Protection

When Stephen finally got up, his father had already gone away for the day. He gave a sigh of relief, for he still felt humiliated from yesterday's experiences. Agnes was getting ready to go wash the laundry in the river. Even though it hurt, Stephen helped lift the heavy basket to her head. Agnes smiled warmly at him as she left the yard.

Madame Gustave brought Stephen a steaming cup of Haitian coffee and a biscuit. She sat down near him. She felt that her son might want to talk.

Stephen really did want to tell his mother the truth. He was bothered by the lies Felix had told his parents. He felt his mother would understand and tell Father what really happened later. So he began to talk.

He told his mother how Fifi had led him into the bushes and dug up the fresh dirt. He said he had no idea that a voodoo sacrifice had been buried there. He told of his curiosity the next day and his thoughts of a buried treasure. He explained how surprised and fearful he was when he recognized that he had uncovered a sacrifice. He even told his mother that Claude had become a Christian. This was surprising news to her.

Stephen felt much better after he talked to his mother. She did understand! She assured him that she would do something to get one of the loa to protect him so something worse wouldn't happen to him. She immediately went into action.

In the rear of the yard was a devil's house; a long, whitewashed building covered with a tin roof. In it were three rooms, side by side. Each room had a door to the outside. Each room had voodoo altars where Stephen's father and mother made offerings to the loa. Around the altars were calabash bowls (scooped-out gourds) in which they placed food for the spirits, multicolored silk flags, and candles. There were all kinds of bottles that held bad-smelling solutions, and brightly painted voodoo drums made of hollowed-out tree trunks covered with goatskins. There were metal cases, swords, wooden bowls, and clay pots.

Madame Gustave was busy the rest of the morning. She prepared what she thought would be a proper offering to the loa in behalf of Stephen. First she killed a large, white chicken and poured its blood into a bowl. Then she prepared a pot of cornmeal, a large plate of herbs, leaves, and cashew nuts. These were all important to make just the right voodoo charms to protect Stephen from the angry loa.

That afternoon Stephen's mother gave him a red undershirt. She tied a strong cord around his waist. It had hundreds of small knots tied in it. She assured her son that he would be safe because a spirit would have

to untie each knot before he could do any harm. But Stephen had to wear the red shirt and cord all the time to be safe. Stephen felt well-protected.

Stephen heard the chatter of voices in the distance. His friends would soon be passing by his house on their way to the soccer game. Stephen hurried inside. He told his mother he didn't want to play soccer today. His back still ached from yesterday's beating, and he was still too embarrassed to see his friends.

No sooner had he gotten out of sight than he heard Claude talking to his mother.

"No, Claude," he heard his mother say. "Stephen isn't here. I don't know what time he'll be home."

Claude sounded disappointed. "Well, tell Stephen I'll be back to see him this evening. I've been thinking about him all day."

Stephen really did want to see Claude. It was the other boys he did not want to see. Since he had told Claude about his problem, he knew his friend understood Felix's actions at the soccer game.

Claude returned late that afternoon. There was a balmy breeze from the sea. The two boys decided to go for a walk. They wanted to be alone so they could talk privately.

"I was really sorry about what happened yesterday," Claude said sincerely. "Did Felix beat you with that whip?"

"No, he let my father do the beating. Didn't you watch with the other fellows?" Stephen asked.

"No, none of us watched. The fellows wanted to,

but I told them not to. I explained a little of the problem, since they were so curious. They all felt bad at the way Felix acted."

Stephen was glad to know that the boys did not watch. He knew that Claude was a true friend. He showed real sympathy and understanding. Claude was certainly different these days!

"Have you heard yet about the services being held by the Christians in Magrit's courtyard?" Claude asked.

"Gospel services . . . in Magrit's yard?" Stephen asked with a shocked tone. "Why? Has Magrit become a Christian too?"

"Not yet," said Claude, "but she's quit a lot of her voodoo practices. She is thinking seriously about Christianity. Anyway, she has agreed to let us hold a gospel service in her yard each week. She even comes to them. We'll be having a service there tomorrow night."

"That's real news!" exclaimed Stephen.

"How about going with me?" asked Claude. "I'd like for you to hear the Christians sing. I'd like for you to hear about Jesus. I've never been so happy before in my life. If you'll become a Christian, Stephen, Jesus will make things different in your life. He'll protect you too. You won't have to be afraid of evil spirits harming you. You won't have to worry anymore about zombies and vampires!"

Stephen had never heard anyone talk this way before. He didn't answer.

"We also learn lots of neat things at the services. I learned how to make water safe to drink and what to do when my little sister gets sick. How about it, Stephen?" Claude asked. "Will you go with me tomorrow night?"

"I'll think about it," replied Stephen.

"I'll be praying for you," Claude said.

Claude was very eager to tell Stephen about Jesus. He not only prayed but also asked his Christian friends, the pastor of the church, and the missionaries to pray too. Everyone prayed for Stephen.

When Stephen went to bed that night, he did a lot of serious thinking. He was confused. What about these voodoo charms his mother had put together for him that day? Could they really protect him? What about Felix? Did the sacrifice really make Felix the sheriff? His mind was filled with doubts. He didn't know what to think. Claude sounded so sure! Stephen wondered if he would ever be as confident as Claude was.

7

A New Experience

The next evening Claude, dressed in his best clothes, stopped by Stephen's house. Stephen was ready to go to the services with him. Claude was delighted.

The two boys climbed the steep hill to Magrit's voodoo courtyard. Stephen could hardly believe that proud, stubborn Magrit would allow Christian activities in her yard. He was really curious to see what would go on. Many times before, he and Claude had climbed this hill to attend the voodoo dances. They had seen Magrit under the spell of the loa—dancing and performing magic.

The yard was swept clean. Magrit had her table brought out and placed under the huge Mapou (mah-POO) tree that is sacred to voodoo. She was dressed in a clean red and white dress and a new, bright head scarf. She carefully spread a fresh tablecloth on the table, arranged each side neatly, and motioned for a little boy to hand her four rocks to hold down each corner. Then she had the little boy carry out chairs for the service.

In the far corner of the yard was a large canopy

with voodoo drums hanging from the ceiling. Behind this was Magrit's devil house—similar to the one in Stephen's yard.

The Christians gathered happily under the huge tree—greeting one another and bowing their heads in prayer. They were thrilled to have the opportunity to sing, teach, and worship in a place like this. Someone began to play an accordion. The Christians sang and clapped their hands in time to the music.

Stephen felt awkward at first, but the warm smiles, greetings, and handshakes from the Christians soon made him feel welcome. They seemed to really care about him and to be glad he was in the service. Never before had he met people who showed such an interest in him.

A smiling young man led the singing. Young people got up and testified between the lively gospel songs and choruses. Everyone seemed so happy as he told what Jesus had done for him personally. Some told how they had paid huge fees to the voodoo priest until they had nothing left—no furniture, no animals, no earthly possessions. Then they found that God could help them and would provide for all their needs.

Stephen watched the expression on Magrit's face. She was listening just as closely as he was. When the Christians sang, Magrit tried to sing along with them. Sometimes she would clap her hands. Stephen enjoyed the service.

When the young pastor got up he told how Jesus had come to help everyone know God's love. But people have sinned—disobeyed God and done wrong things. And instead of being angry, like the loa, God wants to forgive people for the bad things they have done, so they can love Him.

Stephen felt something new inside. He knew he

had done wrong things. He was sorry for them. He wanted God to forgive him.

The Christians started singing again.

Do you want to break the old cords of sin?
> *There's power in Christ's blood; there's power in Christ's blood.*

Do you want to conquer over all wickedness?
> *There's wonderful power in Christ's blood.*

Stephen thought about the cord tied around his waist, the red undershirt he was wearing, and the offering his mother had made to keep away the evil spirits. Now these Christians were offering to him another Protector, Jesus.

A number of chairs were placed in a row in front

of the table that had been used as a pulpit. The pastor invited people to come there to pray. Three young people stepped out from their places and knelt. Claude asked Stephen if he wanted to go pray.

Stephen's heart was beating rapidly. He felt he ought to do something. He hesitated for a moment, then stepped out and knelt at one of the chairs. Claude knelt by his side and put his hand on Stephen's shoulder. Other Christians gathered around to pray. Then for the first time in his life, Stephen prayed. He suddenly felt as though a weight were lifted from his heart. There was peace.

Stephen took off his voodoo charms and gave them to the pastor to burn. Now he would trust Christ to protect him.

As Stephen and Claude walked home that night, the stars seemed especially bright. A full tropical moon lighted the path. The warm breeze rustled through the treetops. The world seemed like a new place to Stephen.

8

A Real Treasure Found

Stephen slept soundly, but some inner clock sounded its alarm long before breakfast. A feeling that there was something important he must do aroused him instantly.

No one else was awake. The sun had barely come up. Stephen quietly slipped outside under the large mango tree in his yard. He opened the Bible that Claude had loaned him and began to read in the Gospel of John. Then he knelt down and prayed. He asked the Lord to help him tell his parents and family about this new Christian way he had found.

When he got up from his knees he saw a tall figure standing in the shadows. It was his father. Stephen wondered how long he had been watching. Perhaps this was a good time to tell what had happened.

Stephen walked toward the house.

With a pleasant smile Stephen said, "*Bonjou* (Good morning), Papa."

Mr. Gustave mumbled, "*Bonjou.*" His face looked stern. "What is the meaning of this, Stephen?"

Stephen thought a moment; then smiling again,

he said, "Papa, something very wonderful happened to me last night. I attended the church service in Magrit's yard. I asked God to forgive all the wrong things I had done."

His father looked stunned by the news. Choosing his words carefully, he said, "Son, why do you meddle in another religion now? You know I have been plan-

ning to train you to be a voodoo priest. What shame do you bring upon us now?"

By this time Madame Gustave was on the porch beside her husband. She, too, looked troubled.

"Is Magrit a Christian?" she asked curiously.

"Not yet," replied Stephen, "but I think she wants to become one."

"And are you a Christian?" Madame Gustave asked.

44

Stephen swallowed hard and then answered. "Yes."

Mr. Gustave said, "Well, you had better change your mind if you plan to stay in this household!" He walked away, very angry.

In the days that followed, Stephen thought much about his father's words. Still he was determined not to give Jesus up. He tried especially hard to please his parents, working hard in the garden. He did extra chores around the house and yard. He was obedient and kind. His family could not help but notice the great change in him.

Stephen talked to Agnes about Jesus every chance he got. The next week she attended the church service. Agnes decided to become a Christian too.

Then one day Mr. Gustave went away on business. Madame Gustave had become so interested in watching the change in Stephen and Agnes that she decided to find out more about Christ. She secretly wanted the same peace and joy her children had.

On Sunday afternoon Stephen rushed to his Christian friends who were out visiting people in the village.

"Come quickly!" he said. "My mother wants to be a Christian!"

Christians from every direction gathered in the Gustaves' yard. From the devil's house, they carried out all the voodoo items and burned them in a bonfire while they sang.

That afternoon Madame Gustave became a Christian. God forgave her for all her voodoo practices.

But what would happen when Mr. Gustave returned home and found the altars destroyed?

No one knew, but God had already begun to talk
to Mr. Gustave. For weeks he had watched Stephen's

life. He had already decided he wanted this new life for himself. He was glad to hear his wife had made the decision first and destroyed the voodoo altars and items.

Stephen called his friends to come pray with his father. And so Stephen's home became a truly Christian home. Mr. and Mrs. Gustave—converted voodoo priest and priestess—became faithful Christians in the village of Fragneau.

Sometimes Stephen smiles when he remembers the "hidden treasure" that he and Fifi dug up—only to find a forbidden voodoo sacrifice. But how happy he is for the real treasure he has found in Christ! It's one that can never be taken away from him—one that will last forever!